We dedicate the book to Howie Schwartz, whose enthusiasm, good humor, and wit made every fishing trip more enjoyable than it deserved to be. Howie's friendship for all of us who fished with him over nearly 30 years was treasured. His creativity was the guiding light behind the founding of Chico Enterprises and the inspiration for this book. Howie got us to think way outside the box and occasionally outside the universe. Plus, he kept us in flies he tied. We miss him tremendously.

We also dedicate this work to our wives who allowed us to travel far and wide in search of finned creatures while they patiently waited for us to return home bearing trinkets from cheap tourist traps. They always feigned surprise and joy at receiving that junk.

Finally, we dedicate this book to those fishermen who, like us, cannot cast like Lefty Kreh, tie flies like Bob Clouser, or know trout like Ernest Schwiebert. We just enjoy being in the outdoors with a rod in hand hoping to catch something other than a cold.

Bill Mandulak   Harry Sadlock   Norm Urmy

Table of Contents

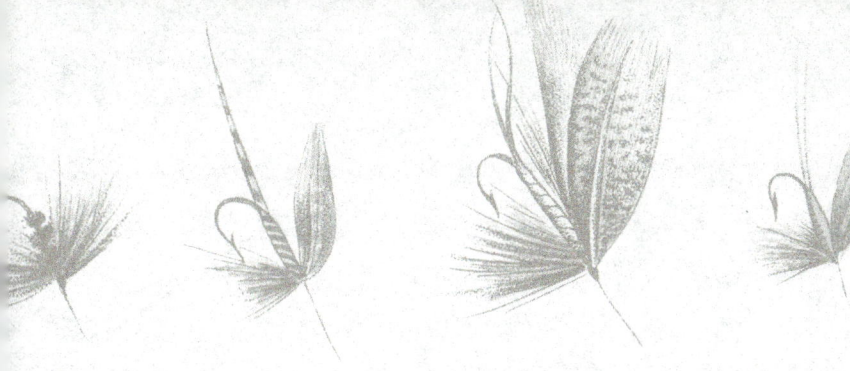

own Palmer. 10. Stone Fly. 11. Grey Drake. 12. Brown Mo

"I FISH BECAUSE I LOVE TO.

12. Brown Moth. 13. Red Spinner. 14. Black Gnat 15. Willow Fly.

7. Jock Scott.

8. Pennell's Pattern.
(Gold Bodied)

TROUT FLIES.

Because I love the environs where trout are found, which are invariably beautiful, and hate the environs where crowds of people are found, which are invariably ugly...Because in a world where most men seem to spend their lives doing what they hate, my fly fishing is at once an endless source of delight and an act of small rebellion. Because trout do not lie or cheat and cannot be bought or bribed, or impressed by power, but respond only to quietude and humility, and endless patience. Because I suspect that men are going this way for the last time and I for one don't want to waste the trip. Because mercifully there are no telephones on trout waters. Because in the woods I can find solitude without loneliness...And finally, not because I regard fly fishing as being so terribly important, but because I suspect that so many of the other concerns of men are equally unimportant and not nearly so much fun."

Robert Traver (John D. Voelker)
Anatomy of a Fisherman

INTRO
DUC
TION

C hico Enterprises was born out of some foolifishness that occurred among a small group of fly fishing buddies after decades of fly fishing trips. Let's call them Howie, Bill, Harry and Norm. (Strangely, their parents called them that too!)

One evening, after a day of fly fishing, while sitting around the dinner table (and later a bar), we were lamenting the fact we needed a way to more affordably pay for our fly fishing trips. In a moment of pure inspiration, we struck upon the ideal approach: form a company whose sole purpose was to develop innovative (although possibly useless) products and services that would allow us to write off the costs. Thus, Chico Enterprises was born.

The company credo:

"The IRS can and should pay for all our fishing trips."

The name, Chico Enterprises, was decided upon after several martinis were consumed while staying at Chico Hot Springs in Pray, Montana. We're pretty sure this happened the same night we snuck over to the restaurant's stereo and replaced some chamber music with a Jerry Jeff Walker concert album.

But none of us can exactly remember for sure...

Chico has the perfect corporate model for those of us who want to fish a lot. We have only executives and board members who are the same people. We have no lengthy meetings or outsiders to answer to. We have no products so we have no production or inventory problems. Since we have only executives and no employees we have no labor / management disagreements. In short we can fish whenever we want!

❋ The purpose of this booklet is neither to educate anyone on the techniques of fly fishing, nor to reveal any secrets (such as special flies, productive rivers, honey holes and the like).

Rather, we hope to present a perspective into fly fishing that inspires you, Dear Reader, to join us in the pure joy and fun of our sport and the idiocy one can enjoy in its pursuit. The information contained in this text was garnered from a cumulative 100+ years of fly fishing. You would think that would make it longer but due to old age we can't remember much of what we've learned. After all, if the success of a fly fishing trip is measured by the number and size of fish caught, we might all do better to stay home and watch television. We believe the success of a fishing trip should be measured by the friendship and laughter shared during the pursuit of those pea-brained fish.

GUIDE SPEAK DE-CODED

As we all know, guides are a necessary part of our fishing experience. They are particularly valuable in waters with which we are unfamiliar or are inaccessible without their employ. That is, we gotta use them! However, they, like politicians, don't always speak clearly. They often use obscure, coded language, not to mislead but, perhaps, to paint a picture not always consistent with the truth. That is to say they lie. So, it's important to understand the true meaning of the words and phrases used by guides. With that, let us begin our translation of "guide speak."

The bull starts with the guide's description of current fishing prospects even before you start fishing.

1

When a guide says,

→ *What he means...*

" **The fishing has been a little tough.** "

is that Ernest Schwiebert on his best day couldn't catch a decent fish under current conditions. The wind is blowing 30+ MPH straight upstream, and the water is freezing in the rod guides.

2

When a guide says,

"**The fishing has been a little slow.**"

→ *What he means...*

is that the conditions are okay, but the average catch per day is less than one. These words should make any fisherman's blood run cold. The guide has set a trap in his statement because he leaves open the possibility that, while fishing has been so bad, God with a gill net couldn't get one, we, with our limited skills, can turn the tide and slay 'em today.

3

When a guide says,

"**The water is a little off color.**"

→ *What he means...*

is that coffee with cream is clearer. Any fly dropped in the water disappears instantly. Only the addition of a live worm would give you a chance!

4

When a guide says,

"We really got 'em yesterday."

→ **What he means...**

is that God smiled on the poor soul he took out. He stumbled onto the perfect fly and they caught one fish every hour or so. Sometimes, the guide will refer to this kind of day as having "steady action." These two terms can be confusing to the uninitiated angler. Don't be. Because no matter which is more accurate for yesterday, your chances of having the same kind of day today are zilch. This is the genesis of the saying, "You should have been here yesterday," the story of our lives.

5

When a guide says,

"Let's see your equipment."

→ **What he means...**

is that he wants to see if your stuff is from Walmart® or Orvis®. He also wants to see if it has ever been used before. Always show him your best rod and reel and make sure it's not brand new. Brand new equipment is a dead giveaway that will relegate you to being thought of as a neophyte, unworthy of a chance at any significant fish.

When a guide says,

" I'll adjust your leader."

→ **What he means...**

is say goodbye to that new fluorocarbon leader as he cuts it in half and complains how poorly the new leaders are made. The best thing to do is to find an old, cheap mono leader and tie it on. Then switch to fluorocarbon when he's cutting up your partner's leader. Always urge your partner to tie on a new fluorocarbon leader. Then you get to laugh.

When a guide says,

" Nice cast ! " or " Good shot ! "

→ **What he means...**

is that you finally got past the front of the boat. Saying this multiple times is a sure sign he is angling for a bigger tip. If you actually catch a fish on a "Nice Cast!" an even bigger tip is expected.
You should ignore the total surprise he exhibits.

8

When a guide says,

→ **What he means...**

" Perfect cast, just leave it!"

is that after hitting everything on the boat, you finally got a decent cast, so don't mess it up now. If you hear this often, hang on to your wallet; this is high grade sucking up.

*Note: The pre-fishing conversation is always important and will be covered in our section on the guide rating system. However, it is crucial here to recognize a couple key phrases the guide may use in arranging the trip.

9

When a guide says,

→ **What he means...**

" Let's meet early to get on the river first."

is that he believes you are such a poor fisherman that unless you get the first crack at the dumb fish, your odds of catching anything go into the toilet along with any tip!

10

When a guide says,

" We can leave a little later to give the water a chance to warm up."

What he means...
is that he has a big night planned for the night before involving heavy drinking. He figures he will be way too hung over to see anything before noon.

11

When a guide says,

" Let's pull over and rest the fish a little while. It will give them a chance to settle down."

What he means...
is that he is so tired of getting your flies out of every snag on the river he needs to soak his arms in ice water.

When a guide says,

"Wow, that's a big fish that rolled on your fly!"

What he means...

is: "you idiot, you missed the fish of the day."

If by chance you actually land a fish,

there are a number of phrases used to describe your trophy. For example, "Really pretty fish!" means you have caught the runt of the litter, but the hatchling's colors are pleasant. "Good average size fish for this place." usually describes a rather puny but alive fish. "Really nice fish!" means you may have actually caught one of legal size. This fish is usually released very quickly so as not to subject it to the embarrassment of measurement. "Big, big fish!" usually means you caught one of average size, but the guide is only sucking up for a tip. This is usually a 'picture fish' that is held with outstretched arms as far as possible toward the camera!

When a guide says,

" Well, it was a beautiful day on the water!"

What he means...

is that he is hoping you enjoyed the trip even though you didn't catch jack shit. This is a phrase used to confuse your thinking in order to bolster his chances of getting a tip. If the guide says, "We gave it our best shot. The fish just weren't in a feeding mood. Your casting was spot on." what he means is that a 4-year-old could cast better than you. This is unabashed brownnosing in the face of utter defeat. Inside guide circles, this is known as the end-of-day "Hail Mary!"

CHOOS-ING A GUIDE

A BETTER WAY

No matter how accomplished an angler you've become, there are always times when a guide is needed. Although most think the primary reason to hire a guide is to increase the chances of actually catching a fish, this is not always true. Often, we have found it is simply necessary to have someone to blame for our poor fishing results There are many options available for choosing a guide. Unfortunately, all of them are based ninety-eight percent on opinion, fallible memory, and/or blatant deceit.

The method that is most often employed is personal experience: you can choose to hire a guide you have fished with before. This relies heavily on your memory of those previous experiences, which we all know can fade and distort over time, especially if the experience was a decent one. When rebooked, it's likely our results with the guide will fall way short of expectations. Of course we eliminate rehiring guides who have been unsuccessful in putting us on fish.

A second approach is to ask other fishermen for advice. Fishing friends are always willing to provide suggestions about "great" guides. But here's the problem: since all fishermen are basically liars, their advice has to be taken with a huge grain of salt; it's just not realistic to believe that a fisherman who's had a great experience will tell us the truth.

They always jealously guard any information that helped them have a great fishing experience. How many honey holes have **YOU** divulged to another fisherman?

None, right?

Another obvious solution in this modern age is the Internet. There's some useful information floating on the Internet concerning guides. As we have great faith in the veracity of all things on the Internet, this can be a helpful resource...as long as *Snopes* can verify it. You can't be too careful.

Angling publications offer another source for guide selection. Guides who publish articles are usually viewed as "experts," but, frankly, we feel they are mostly just clever writers and, as mentioned above, liars (reread the chapter on "guide speak" for more on this). Some publications have even gone so far as to make awards for guides. These awards are often categorized as "Guide of the Year" or "Top Ten Guides" of the year. And on and on. We suggest these guides be avoided at all costs. Hiring a thusly decorated guide will virtually eliminate any possibility of blaming them for a poor day on the water.

Finally, a call to one or more tackle shops can be useful in identifying guides when fishing new water.

The obvious issue with this approach is that the shops usually get a percentage of the guide fee from those guides who work with them. So, they're only going to name the ones who give them a kickback, regardless of their skill or knowledge as guides. However, if you feel you must go this route, we suggest calling well in advance and, using several fictitious dates, inquire as to which guides are available. Those who are consistently available must NOT be hired since they obviously have no following in the knowledgeable fishing community. All you have to do then is hire the guide who is never available - a guide fishing "Catch 22."

There is a Better Way!

As asserted previously, the standard methods for finding and choosing your guide are all significantly flawed and will inevitably lead to an unsatisfactory or mediocre experience... unless you just luck out through some fortunate twist of fate. What we all need is an objective, evidence-based and data-driven way to find that excellent, helpful, friendly, and knowledgeable guide. Rejoice! That system is available to you now! History will record this solution as one of the major innovations of Chico Enterprises.
- The **F**lyfishers **I**nteractive **G**uide **E**xcellence **R**ating **S**ystem (**F.I.G.E.R.S.**)!

F. I. G. E. R. S.

Flyfishers
Interactive
Guide
Excellence
Rating
System

F.I.G.E.R.S. has been developed through 100 collective years' experience of hiring and judging guides by the executive team at Chico Enterprises. F.I.G.E.R.S. is a system that can be used by all serious anglers. Using the system's critical measures of guide performance, clear and unambiguous evaluative data on all guides can be collected in real-time and added to our web site database by any angler (as soon as we figure out how to build a web site database). F.I.G.E.R.S. is a complete system covering not only the basics of finding and catching fish, but including all the elements that make a day on the water more enjoyable. F.I.G.E.R.S. is scientific, objective, real-time, and actually useful!

Before delving into the astounding details of F.I.G.E.R.S., we need to lay the groundwork for you. The guided fly fishing trip is logically divided into six natural segments.

1 **Booking and Pre-Trip Discussion:** During this phase you will meet the guide (usually by phone) and discuss the trip, your hopes and objectives, and arrive at a tentative plan for the day.

2 **The Meet:** This is the time you arrive at the fly-shop or outfitter's and actually meet your guide face-to-face. Additional details of the day are usually worked out in this phase. Pre-fishing banter (PFB) is an important dynamic in this phase.

3 **Pre-Launch:** This phase includes the ride to the put in and the setting up of your gear (rods, leaders, initial flies, etc.). Conversation allowing you and your guide to get to know each other and further refine the plans for the day is held.

4 **The Float/Wade — pre & post lunch:** Now you're actually fishing and having that all-important interaction with the guide on the water. Before lunch, you're getting to know your guide, and after, you're applying the lessons gleaned from the morning. You're taking your angler-guide collaboration to the next level.

5 **Lunch:** That time period where R & R happens, including some assessment of your morning, some grub, perhaps a hit or two from your flask, and a stogie.

6 **Takeout/Return to Car and Ride Home:** The fishing day is done. Assessments of the day with your guide are made and the guide's tip is determined (if any). You pack up and head for home while making decisions about another float/wade.

NOTE: Each segment must be thoroughly evaluated on its own to arrive at that perfect guide evaluation score needed to judge and compare guides over time. Armed with this amazingly complete data set, you, dear angler, can always, with complete confidence, pick and hire the best guide available! Wouldn't that just be amazing?
Of course it would.

What follows is the standard F.I.G.E.R.S. evaluation score sheet. It is divided into the logical sections as laid-out above. Key evaluation guidelines, data points, and criteria are delineated for each time period, along with suggested, or, in some instances, mandated, point ranges or scores. It is highly recommended that you advise your guide that you will be using F.I.G.E.R.S. during the day. We've found guide performance improves dramatically when you do this! The occasional negative reaction usually means an unpleasant trip. If your guide is unfamiliar with F.I.G.E.R.S., you're gonna have some fun unveiling it throughout the day, announcing key scores as you go. Of course, care must be taken with this approach as it could set unrealistic expectations for a large tip, or, conversely, a long walk home.

✱ IMPORTANT NOTE TO GUIDES:

Guides, don't despair as you contemplate being exposed as the awesome or awful guide that you are. Soon, you will also be able to take control in deciding, with objective data, just who you will or will not guide. No more chance or random guiding encounters with sports you wish you could send to the bottom of the river with lead core line wrapped around their neck! Finally, a reliable way to ensure every client you serve is an easygoing, friendly fisherperson who can cast like Lefty Kreh, brings his or her own gear (and flies), and tips like a millionaire. GROSS is the answer! That is, the Guide's Rating Of Sports System. Chico's crack development team is hard at work bringing this dream of every guide into reality. Stay tuned, guides of the world - help is on the way!

The Score Sheet:

The Booking:

- Does guide know the water you want to fish that day? **Yes: Score 1-10 points**

- Has guide heard of your desired fish species? **Yes: Score 1- 10 points**

- Does guide suggest best tackle & flies? **Yes: Score 1-50 points**

- Does guide mention worms? **Yes: Minus 10 points**

- Does guide mention spin lures? **Yes: Minus 10 points**

- Does guide mention bobbers? **Yes: Minus 2 points**

- Does guide say to bring your own life jacket? **Yes: Minus 25 points**

- Does bail get mentioned? **Yes: Minus 50 points OR maybe plus 50, depending on the contemplated offense.**

- Does Guide say is noon too early to meet and start trip? **Yes: Minus 50 points**

- Does guide ask what you want for lunch on the trip day? **No: Minus 50 points**

Section Total: _____

The Meet:

- Does guide engage in banter? **Yes: Score 1-20 points**

- Does guide exhibit good sense of humor? **Yes: Score 1-20 points**

- Does guide laugh at your jokes? **Yes: Score 1-20 points**

The Meet (continued):

• Does guide know they are jokes? **Yes: Score 1-20 points**

• Can guide stand good-natured kidding? **Yes: Score 1-10 points**

• Does guide share good stories about fishing? **Yes: Score 1-10 points**

• About his/her sex life? **No: Score 1-10 points**

• Can guide keep up with banter without you explaining it? **Yes: Score 1-5 points**

• Does guide react negatively to your using FIGERS? **Yes: Minus 50 points**

Section Total:

Pre-Launch:

• Does guide change out your new tippet for one of his/hers? **Yes: Minus 10 points**

• Does guide help set up your rig for the launch? **Yes: Score 1-15 points**

• Does guide break your rod during setup? **Yes: Minus 1,000 points**

• Does guide suggest best flies for the day? **Yes: Score 1-15 points**

• Did guide know how to get to launch ramp? **No: Minus 50 points**

• Does guide continue banter during ride to ramp? **Yes: Score 1-25 points**

• Does guide ask how you like to fish? **Yes: Score 1-15 points**

• Does guide use confusing lingo, like hexagenia limbata, or pseudocleon? **Yes: Minus 10 points**

• Does guide use lingo like "really big brown flies" or "little green flies"? **Yes: Score 1-20 points**

Section Total:

The Float/Wade - pre and post lunch:

- Does guide carry a good selection of flies? **Yes: Score 1-20 points**

- Does guide ask you to use your flies? **Yes: Minus 20 points**

- Does guide keep your flies after changing them out? **Yes: Minus 50 points**

- Is guide willing to row or maneuver boat to retrieve your flies when snagged or hung up:

  - The first time? **Score 1-15 points**

  - The second time? **Score 15-20 points**

  - The third time? **Score 20-25 points**

- At what snag number does your guide quit retrieving the hung fly & say: "Break it off"?

  - 5: **Score 5 points**

  - 8: **Score 15 points**

  - 12: **Score 100 points**

- Does guide compliment you on the speed of your hook set? **Yes: Score 1-10 points**

- Does guide criticize the speed of your hook set (when fly is pulled from fish's mouth)?
  Yes: Minus 25 points

- Does guide compliment your LDR's (Long Distance Releases)? **Yes: Score 1-15 points**

- Does guide ridicule your LDRs? **Yes: Minus 20 points**

- Does guide compliment your SDRs (Short Distance Release)? **Yes: Score 1-15 points**

- Does guide cause SDRs (bad netting technique, etc.)? **Yes: Minus 20 points**

The Float/Wade - (continued):

• Does guide take extraordinary measures to land your fish? **Yes: Score 1-50 points**

• Does the guide say things like: "Not like that, you idiot?" Or roll his/her eyes?
Yes: Minus 50 points

• Will guide take pictures of your nice fish? Hold them for you? **Yes: Score 1-10 points**

• Does guide suggest holding fish close to camera to make it look bigger than it is?
Yes: Plus 50 points

• Does guide put fish in his/her box for his/her dinner that night? **Yes: Minus 30 points**

• Does guide engage in on-stream banter (OSB)? **Yes: Score 1- 50 points**

• Does guide say nice things, like: "Nice Shot!" or "Good Cast!" and often?
Yes: Score 1-300 points

• Did your guide tie all your flies on for you? **Yes: Score 1-50 points**

• Did any guide knots fail while setting the hook, playing a fish, or landing a fish?
Yes: Minus 50 points per failure

• Did your guide mock you when you had a SAM (Stung And Missed fish)?
Yes: Minus 10 points per mockery

• Did the guide run out of the fly(ies) that have been slaying the fish?
Yes: Minus 150 points

• Did your guide say: "Get 'em!" all day (indicating a need for a hit of Fast-Strike...see product catalog)? **Yes: Minus 10 points per utterance**

Section Total: _____

Lunch:

- Did guide ask you to bring your own lunch? **Yes: Minus 100 points**

- Does lunch include Chicken Cordon Bleu, or just sandwiches? **Score 1-50 points**

- Is lunch cold or is it hot? **Score 1-50 points**

- Are drinks provided?

  - Water only: **Minus 20 points**

  - Also soda: **Plus 10 points**

  - Also Jack Daniels®: **Plus 150 points**

- Is there dessert?

  - None: **Minus 50 points**

  - Cookies: **Plus 10 points**

  - Cookies and a candy bar: **Plus 25 points**

  - Twinkies®: **Plus 100 points**

- Does guide provide time for a post lunch cigar? **Yes: Plus 35 points**

- Did the guide complain about cigar smokers? **Yes: Minus 100 points**

- If in States where legal, is cannabis provided?

  - **Yes: Plus 1,500 points**

  - **Yes and munchies: Plus 2,000 points**

- Did your guide borrow your rod during lunch and show off his/her casting prowess?
  - **Yes: Minus 150 points**

Lunch (continued):

• Did he/she catch a fish while you ate? **Yes: Minus 100 points**

• Did he/she catch the biggest fish of the day in front of you?

• Yes: Minus 550 points and possibly no tip

• Did guide offer entertainment (jokes) during lunch?

• Yes: Plus 10 points

• Funny jokes you can use: Plus 50 points

• Dirty jokes that are funny: Plus 100 points

• Dirty, hilarious sex jokes: Plus 200 points

Section Total:

The Takeout and Return Home:

• Did you catch any fish? **Yes: Score 1-250 points**

• Any really nice ones? More than one? **Yes: Score 1- 300 points**

• Did you hook the fish of a lifetime? And land it? Did guide cause you to lose it?

• Yes & landed: Plus 1,000 points

• Yes & lost: Minus 1,000 points

• Yes & landed and released after estimating it as a world record:

Plus 2,000 points and big tip

• Did the guide cause you to fall overboard by his/ her poor boat control?

• Yes: Minus 1,000 points

The Takeout and Return Home (continued):

- Did the guide risk his/her life to rescue you? **Yes: Plus 300 points**

- Did you get the "munchies" (only in states where recreational weed is legal) and some

  chocolate? **Yes: Plus 100 points**

- Will the guide ever speak to you again? **No: Minus 300 points**

- Would you recommend this guide to a friend? **Yes: Score 1-50 points**

- Did the guide give you his/her card? Is it his/hers? **Yes: Plus 20 points**

- Would you recommend this guide to an enemy? **Yes: Minus 150 points**

- Did the guide utter any "Guide Speak" during your entire time of interaction?

  - **Yes: Minus 25 points per utterance**

Section Total: _____

Grand Total: _____

Note*

Should you need more rating sheets,
just buy more books. We need the money.

Rating & Conclusions:

Points:	
-3,000 to -1,000	Worst trip of your life! Consider drowning this guide and stealing his/her boat as compensation for your suffering.
-999 to Zero:	Avoid this guide at all costs. Recommend only to your enemies. Never tip.
Zero to +999	Don't book this guide again. Tip optional. Marginal experience, at best.
+1,000 to +2,500	Had a darn good day. Book again. Recommend to friends. Modest tip.
Above 2,500	Really fantastic trip! Book again for sure. Big tip. Don't tell anyone about this guide. Keep him/her for yourself.

IN STRUC- TIONAL ADVICE

While we at Chico Enterprises have limited skills and almost no evidence we can actually catch fish (except during late night visits to State hatcheries), we nevertheless feel we have a responsibility to share some of our limited knowledge with the even less skilled among you. Why would we do this? Fly fishing has a certain mystique that frightens away many would-be anglers from enjoying the frustrations of this sport. So, we enter the fray to teach little known or unacknowledged techniques that have aided us in our climb to the lower echelons of fly fishing. This will be a short chapter.

The Tailing Loop Cast

The so-called "tailing loop cast" is a cast that has, for many years, been much maligned. In fact, this cast is very easy to execute and comes naturally to many flycasters. The tailing loop is simply made on the back cast by allowing the fly line, leader, and fly to fall below the intended line of the forward cast (or is it the opposite?). Occasionally the fly will hit the fly line and cause a tangle. Not to worry as this can be cured by tipping the rod sidewise (we think). The major advantage of the tailing loop is the fly line usually smashes into the water much earlier than the fly and with a lot more force as well. This action of fly line and fly apparently causes a commotion on the water that stupid fish cannot resist. They hear the commotion and look up to hopefully find your fly. And wham! Another fish on...

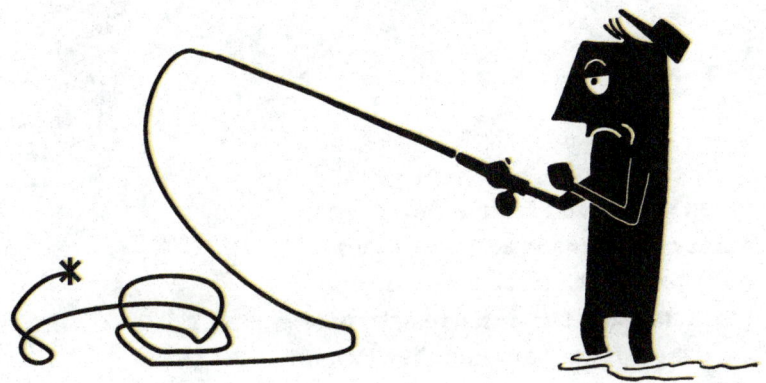

The Puddle Cast

The puddle cast is one rarely mentioned in the major fly-casting instructional tomes. The puddle cast is made by making a weak back cast followed by an even weaker forward cast causing the fly line, leader, and fly to end up in a pile, or "puddle," at the end of the cast. Like the tailing loop cast, the puddle cast concentrates the fish-attracting disturbance around the fly. The challenge in the use of the puddle cast is that it is often difficult to set the hook, as there is always a lot of, let's call it, slack in the line.

The Helen Keller

Helen Keller was a famous American author, lecturer and activist who was both deaf and blind. These are often characteristics attributed to us by guides even though we are neither. The Helen Keller is one of the simplest and yet most effective fly fishing techniques we have ever encountered. If a fly fishermen claims they have never used or caught a fish using this technique, you know you have met a liar. But, hey, we fish, so we DO lie!

The Helen Keller is executed at the end of a cast by simply putting the fly rod under your arm, letting the fly drag in the water, and doing something else. That's right – do not pay attention because fish know when you aren't paying attention (lighting a cigar can really improve the illusion). Now, this is when the magic occurs: while you are not paying attention as intently as possible with the rod under your arm, the fish bites. You have done a perfect Helen Keller!

Trolling-In-Your-Waders

Fly fishermen everywhere use trolling-in-your-waders. It was developed out of the salmon fishing technique of "skating-the-fly." The technique is often masked by knowledgeable fishermen claiming they were just wading to a different spot. We know better. Trolling-in-your-waders is a very purposeful way of catching wary fish. The fly is left to dangle at the end of the fly line, usually further than you could possibly cast. Do not put the rod under your arm as in the Helen Keller because you are attentive to catching a fish. Simply begin to wade away from the spot you were in. Trolling-in-your-waders combines two effective payoffs: The fly has a new action much like the skating fly retrieve and more importantly, (and this is critical and takes a whole lot of practice), the fish see you leaving and falsely sense you are not paying attention. Being casual in your wading makes the illusion perfect.

The Usefulness of the Wind Knot

No single knot has been so vilified in fly fishing circles as the Wind Knot. Yet, the skill required to tie a proper Wind Knot during the act of casting is of the highest order. Imagine tying a proper knot in a line traveling nearly 50 miles per hour (this is just a guess). Of course the skill of the caster must be augmented by just the proper amount of wind – thus the name Wind Knot. The reason it's covered here is to address the utility of the knot.

Say, for example, you need a 7X tippet (2 lb. test) in a given situation but all you have is 6X (4 lb. test). By using the 6X tippet and tying a Wind Knot you now have the proper strength tippet! The Wind Knot is also useful in replacing a fly since you can easily break the tippet at the knot and tie on the new fly. The Wind Knot is also valuable in identifying the proper location to add a new piece of leader material. No need to guess…just break the line at the Wind Knot and add the new leader material. Of course, if the Wind Knot is in the fly line itself, you'll need further instruction… or you could simply try spin fishing.

THE CHICO PRODUCT CATALOG

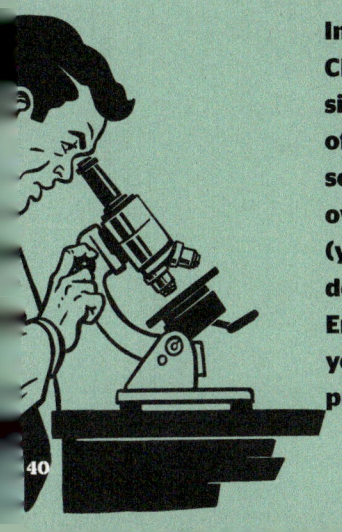

Inventions are the heart and soul of Chico Enterprises. They are the core and single source of its raison d'etre: writing off all fishing trip expenses! In fact, the seeds of the company were planted over a few martinis when the founders, (yup, same Howie, Bill, Harry and Norm), developed their thoughts on the first Chico Enterprises' product. Over the subsequent years, several exciting and innovative product ideas have been conceived.

The AMAZING Contact Lens Finder

The first invention of the fledgling Chico Enterprises came out of a common tragedy of its day and the need for its prevention. The tragedy occurred when Bill dropped one of his contact lenses while cleaning it at the Chico Hot Springs Hotel. Even after many minutes of crawling on the bathroom floor searching, it was never be found. The creative juices, aided by the inspirational, lubricating liquids known as "cocktails" (and possibly wine?), began to flow that night. The solution was pure genius: impregnate contact lenses with a fluorescing compound sensitive to a unique wavelength of light, generated by a special flashlight powered by batteries available only from Chico Enterprises (at an exorbitant price of course). That way, when a lens was dropped, one would only need light up the flashlight, and voila!, the lens would easily be seen, saving contact lens wearer time and money. Sadly, when ready to prototype our new lens, we found they also fluoresced in sunlight, blinding the wearer! Also, unfortunately, disposable contact lenses negated the need to find a dropped lens. Our market opportunity was gone.

Note: Since the lost lens tragedy and the ensuing Lens Finder invention occurred at the renowned Chico Hot Springs Hotel and was the first inspired angler aid, the name Chico Enterprises was adopted.

Never-Break Fly Tippets

Our next product idea was to make fishing line, primarily tippets, out of Kevlar. These tippets could be made extremely thin yet very strong. Even the most incompetent fisherman would never break off another fish. The research we did, mostly on the Internet, revealed that Kevlar, when extruded to very thin diameters, sinks like a rock. Crestfallen, Chico's Board was forced to remove its Never-Break Fly Tippet from the catalog. Undaunted, we are exploring the exciting application that braided spider-web filament could offer fly fishers world-wide. Not all is lost... another opportunity for more martinis!

The Attractant Glove

A product that has reached the prototype stage and could well be a winner, if certain fascist fisheries agencies would allow it, is The Attractant Glove. The notion is to creatively expand the use of fish attractants into multiple applications. The first product that was actually "prototyped" was a special glove with an attractant dispenser integrated into it. The goal is to confuse and outwit those enforcement agents, not to mention simplify and facilitate the use of said attractants. To verify that this was not "cheating," we contacted a noted doctor in the fishing world, Dr. Juice, who verified and reinforced our claim that this was definitely not "cheating."

ALL DISCONTINUED
Attractant Products Galore!

After our discussion with Dr. Juice (and several more martinis), a light bulb went off. Why not combine attractants with other products? The possibilities were vast! Naturally, we targeted fly fishermen first as they will buy nearly any substance or gadget that comes on the market. If you don't believe this, just look in their vests.

We started with attractant in fly tying head cement. From there, mixing fish attractant with sunscreen was a natural follow-up product. Imagine protecting your skin at the same time you draw fish to you. After trying various formulas, we determined this product might best be limited to freshwater, where size and tooth count of the fish is manageable. In saltwater you'd be a walking chum bag!

Other combinations presented themselves, including attractant and mosquito repellent. But this also repelled any hatches on the stream with the obvious impact of turned-off fish. The trade-off was judged not worth it.

Slow-Strike & Fast-Strike

The research on fish attracting chemicals led us into the netherworld of drugs – not just martinis, but pills which would enhance our fish-hooking skills. Two such products were "Slow–Strike" and "Fast–Strike."

"SLOW-STRIKE" is a product needed when a fisherman is too quick setting the hook, particularly when fishing dry flies. The idea is to slow one's reaction time to give the fish the necessary time to inhale the offering. This was to be a fast-acting inhalant with a limited therapeutic time span to facilitate matching the angler's needs with conditions on the stream. We considered several drugs, but with the legalization of marijuana in several states, we felt it was inevitable our product would suffer at the hands of this competition. Leave it to the hippie-liberal voters to ruin a good business idea.

"FAST-STRIKE" proved to be a valuable product for those of us who suffered the opposite affliction: hook-setting reflexes are too slow, and caffeine alone was insufficient to improve reaction time. Those quick-nibbling little trout wouldn't stand a chance! Little did we appreciate the difficulty in securing large enough quantities of stimulant from our local "supplier" to make the venture economically viable (not to mention overcoming certain legal hurdles).

The Hatch-O-Meter

Have you ever been driving alongside a stream or across one on a bridge to find your car engulfed in a cloud of insects suddenly impaled on your windshield by the thousands. A hatch is on! But is it one that'll turn the fish on? Enter Chico's ultimate invention: The Hatch-O-Meter. This is a space-age windshield hatch analyzer that could be the most useful tool in the history of fly fishing. The notion here is to eliminate the need for developing the kind of encyclopedic knowledge of entomology found in Ernest (don't call me Ernie) Schwiebert's great tome "Trout," in addition to saving the angler time on-stream.

THE (STANDARD MODEL) HATCH-O-METER

attaches to the windshield of your car. Using proprietary hardware and software, it detects each insect that hits the windshield and, using a lightning-fast, miniature DNA analyzer, determines the presence of meaningful hatches. The identified insects are then listed on the dashboard mounted LED screen or sent via Bluetooth to your smartphone.

THE (DELUXE MODEL) HATCH-O-METER has

a much faster processor and provides many more user functions. It allows the angler to set hatch density thresholds and issue alerts when they are reached. It lists insect types, in order of relative frequency, on the LED or smartphone. Finally, it suggests appropriate fly patterns and sizes to properly match the hatch in descending order of the most likely to be eaten by the fish. This eliminates the need to read "Selective Trout," "Ring of the Rise," or "Trout Flies of the West."

Chico's latest version (possibly available for Christmas 2023) is The (Streamside) Hatch-O-Meter. This model attaches to a smartphone and comes with a laser sensor. You merely point the laser at the fly the fish are feeding on and it instantly identifies the fly and the appropriate imitation. Early tests were very positive with the exception being if the laser is aimed at the fly but happens to hit the fish – oops, no need for a frying pan! The Chico team has decided more design work and testing is needed on this model due to this major problem - aiming error - encountered during R & D.

UNDER DEVELOPMENT

The Drone Caster

We have suffered much criticism from guides and other fly fishermen concerning a mythical cast called the "tight loop". After much research and endless reviewing of Lefty Kreh videos, we determined the so-called "tight loop" cast to be unattainable by mere mortals. We turned our attention to the notion of using emerging drone technology as an answer. Much to our delight, this proved to be an avenue of considerable promise. Thus was born The Drone Caster. The device is a simple drone with a release mechanism to which the fly line, leader, and fly are attached. The controls, mounted on the butt of the rod, direct The Drone Caster over the intended target and release the fly line, leader, and fly in the perfect spot. Voila! No more need for the "tight loop" or any other kind of loop. In fact, with the proper release, flies could be placed in areas once thought impossible to reach with a cast. Take that Lefty Kreh! We also determined that by managing the Drone Caster effectively the fly could be dappled or drifted on the water. In early tests with seasoned drone control teenagers, the miracle of the "drag free float" was achievable virtually anywhere on a river regardless of varied currents! Imagine the bonanza for inept fly fishermen like us who could now catch virtually any fish.

The description above is of the basic model. A more advanced model would not only achieve the drag free float but also set the hook when that trophy fish hit the fly. The super deluxe model would marry the advanced model with an onboard camera that would send pictures back to the Stream Side Hatch-O-Meter for selection of the perfect fly. Then The Drone Caster could position the fly over the biggest fish in the water and drift a drag free floated fly on his head. The Drone Caster would come in several colors including clear plastic economy model, sky blue, forest green, pink (for women and Californians), camo (for NASCAR fans), and stealth fluorocarbon for particularly spooky fish. And it will be compliant with new FAA regs!

The Fur Finder

As fly fishing gains popularity, it's increasingly difficult to find natural materials for the proper tying of specific fly patterns. Here, technology mates with good old-fashioned tools. The Fur Finder is the answer. The Fur Finder marries a simple animal trap, a smartphone, and a Go-Pro-style camera. The smartphone is loaded with a propriety app and is connected to the camera via Bluetooth. This allows identification of animals as they approach the trap. If the animal matches that which is needed, the trap springs. If no match, the animal is left to pass. So, if you need the urine stained belly fur of a kit fox, just program it into the app and - voila! - you trap the fox. Now you can now tie a perfect Hendrickson fly! (Of course you have to kill the fox).

The Chico Wet Wading System

The Chico board regrets that none of us can remember what the hell this dynamic and revolutionary system actually is or can accomplish.

The Portable Camp Bathtub

Ditto.

The F.I.G.E.R.S. App

Do you like Chico's F.I.G.E.R.S. System? Of course you do! Well, you're really going to like our soon-to-be-released F.I.G.E.R.S. app. This handy-dandy app for your iPhone or Android actually makes using F.I.G.E.R.S. a total breeze. It's perfect for real-time, on-stream, mid-float scoring using Chico's acclaimed guide rating system. Upload scores as you go during the float or wade trip using Chico's patented, voice-activated entry system. You can tell your guide he or she just scored big (or blew it) while at the same time entering the score into F.I.G.E.R.S. Think how helpful it'll be to provide your guide a running total score as the day progresses. What a motivator for the guide to pick up his or her game in helping you have the day of your fly fishing life (or not).

The Chico Cath

Have you ever been on the stream surrounded by members of the opposite sex, or in your belly boat far from shore and heard the "call of nature"? Of course you have! Probably multiple times during each day of fishing. You head for shore, find a spot, put up your rod, take off the vest, undo and lower those waders, take care of business, then reverse the whole process to get back to fishing. Well, those annoying routines are OVER! The Chico Cath will allow you to fish CONTINUOUSLY all day! This miniature, easy-to-don device will monitor your bladder pressure and allow full, hands-free release into the stream or lake where fishermen and fisherwomen know it belongs. Pre-order your Chico Cath today by calling PISS ENDERS (747-736-3377). Specify male or female model, please.

The Chico Rod Warmer

We've all had those days when the cold wind blows, ice forms on your rod guides, and your hands cannot make a decent cast due to the heavy gloves needed to prevent frost bite. Well along comes the Chico Rod Warmer. This little beauty attaches to any rod and is powered by two 9-volt ion alkaline batteries. The heater wires wrap around the handle of your rod to warm your casting hand (should be used with cork only) and then attach to each rod guide to eliminate icing. The proper power adjustment is critical as too little can merely accelerate frostbite and too much will result in severe shock to the hand (particularly if it is wet). Tragically, this will possibly melt your nice graphite rod as our early tests demonstrated. (We'll miss that $900 Thomas and Thomas rod). On the bright side however, we found in our testing if two people are using The Chico Rod Warmer in close proximity and they plunge their rods into the water simultaneously, a "shocking" event occurs. This event numbs the fish and they can easily be scooped up with a hand dip net. This eliminates the need for overpriced rods, expensive lines, and miniscule flies. In fact, complicated casting techniques are no longer neccesary. Of course, good netting skills are needed however! A third person may be required to join in on particularly fast moving water, but the more the merrier. We found the 12-volt car battery models are most effective in this mode, though car batteries are less portable than 9-volt batteries and require a significant backpack for on-stream use. Naturally, the fish are only slightly stunned, which is consistent with a proper conservation ethic. However, if you are using this method of fishing, you probably aren't a catch and release person. We have been led to believe this may also be illegal in a few states in the north (but well accepted in the south).

CHICO'S NEAR PER- FECT- DAY- LONG MENU

(The Only Really Useful Part of This Booklet!)

As we've aged, Chico's Executive Team's on-stream time has decreased. Naturally, this has allowed us more time to pursue other pleasures: drinking and eating. After adding extra martinis, we turned to cooking. The following menu provides the best fruits of those labors. Enjoy!

Breakfast:

· Chico Bloody Mary Mix (Howie's Recipe)

Mix together: 56 oz. low sodium V8, 1/4 oz. Worcestershire Sauce , 1/4 oz. Tabasco
Sauce, 1/2 oz. Angostura Bitters, 1 1/2 tablespoons of celery salt, 2 tablespoons of
salt and 1 tablespoon of black pepper. Add vodka to taste and serve with the juice
of 1/2 lime or wedge.

· Chico's Nutmeg Creamy French Toast

Cut a loaf of challah or brioche bread into 3/4-inch-thick slices. Arrange slices in a
single layer on a sided cookie sheet. Whisk 5 eggs plus 3 egg yolks and 1/4 teaspoon
of salt until frothy. Whisk in 1 cup of half & half, 1/2 cup of plain yogurt, 3 tablespoons
of granulated sugar, and 2 teaspoons nutmeg until well-blended. Pour the mixture
over the bread. Cover with plastic wrap and put in the refrigerator overnight. Turn
bread slices once or twice to assure fully soaked with the egg mixture. Cook on a
medium griddle until brown on the outside and soft inside. Dust with powdered
sugar and serve.

Lunch:

· Your Favorite Sandwich, Cookies and Drink

Come on y'all! You'll be fishing, so cooking's out. You or your guide should pick up
something good at the sandwich shop.

Dinner:

· The Chico Martini (Howie's Again!)

Fill an atomizer with Lillet Light, 3 drops of lemon juice, 3 drops of Angostura Bitters and mix well. Spray three times into your martini shaker, add 3-4 oz. of Gin or Vodka and shake well. Pour into a chilled martini glass and add the garnish of your choice...olives, lemon twist, etc.

· Chico's Marinated Pork Tenderloin

Combine 1/4 cup of soy sauce, 1/4 cup of brown sugar, 2 tablespoons of sherry, 1 1/2 teaspoons of dried and minced onion, 1 teaspoon of ground cinnamon, 2 tablespoons of olive oil and a pinch of garlic powder in a large zip-lock bag. Place pork in the bag, seal and refrigerate for 6 to 12 hours. When ready to cook, bring meat to room temperature. Preheat oven to 400 degrees Fahrenheit. Preheat oiled iron skillet to very hot. Remove tenderloin from bag (discard marinade) and sear on all sides in skillet (4-6 minutes total). Remove to a roasting pan and roast in the oven or until the internal temperature is 145 degrees Fahrenheit. Remove from oven and rest for 10 minutes. Slice and serve.

· Chico's Beef Tenderloin

Bring meat to room temperature. Trim all fat and silver skin. Wrap each 6-8 oz. or 1 1/2-inch-thick tenderloin tournedos in a strip of bacon. Fasten with 3-4 toothpicks. Season with ample amount of salt and pepper. Place 3-4 tablespoons of butter in a cool iron skillet, then turn to high heat. When butter turns brown, drop meat into skillet. Cook tenderloin for 5 minutes per side for very rare, 5 1/2 minutes for rare, etc. Turn only once! Rest for 5 minutes. Serve. If any of your guests ask for bottled steak sauce, take their tenderloin away and serve them a burger (or ask them to leave).

Dinner (Continued):

· Chico's Baked Potato Wedges

Wash and slice 4 russet potatoes into six equal lengthwise wedges. Place slices in a bowl of water with 2 cups of ice cubes for 30 minutes. Remove and pat dry. Mix 1/4 teaspoon of salt, 1/4 teaspoon of garlic powder, 1/4 teaspoon of paprika and 1/4 teaspoon of black pepper in a large zip-lock bag. Add potatoes and shake. Add 1/4 cup of olive oil and toss. Place the potatoes on a parchment paper lined baking sheet and bake in a 450 degree preheated oven until cooked thru, browned and crispy. Garnish with parsley and Parmesan cheese

· The Chico Dessert and Nightcap

Dessert is always a challenge. So many great choices! We have learned over the years that a dram or two of single malt, rye or sour mash goes a long way in wrapping things up and preparing us for the next day of angling. Due to our age and intolerance for calories, we have strayed from those cakes, pies and cookies. However, an occasional scoop of good ice cream helps the nightcap go down.

Final Thoughts

The Executive Team wishes you good water and tight lines! May you and your guides remain liars for all eternity, and, may you never achieve the Chico Grand Slam.

Huh? Wait a minute! What's that?

The Grand Slam is when the angler manages to lose a fly on a single guided trip in all four of the following ways: on a rock, on a tree, on a fish and on a person. If that person is your guide, you've managed to achieve a Super Grand Slam, as guides are shifty devils and have learned to avoid being hooked (much like the fish). The current Chico record is a quadruple Grand Slam.

Buck up Anglers! We hope this booklet has brought a smile to your face or a chuckle to your belly. We wish you fine martinis and stogies in the evenings after a happy and productive day on the water with friends.

CHEERS!

CPSIA information can be obtained
at www.ICGtesting.com
Printed in the USA
FSOW03n0550190317
31811FS